You Can't Shit Yourself on a Bicycle....

..And other handy travel tips!

Jo Lomas

To Becca,

May all your travels be full of fun & laughter

love you

JoLo
xxx

Contents

Introduction   v

1. Don't be Shy.... of squat toilets and Bum guns   1
2. Don't Take the Piss.... with a she-wee and butterflies   9
3. Don't Wear.... white trousers on a cave tour   13
4. Don't Run another Man's Race...when you can't even jog   17
5. Don't Swallow it All.... especially when invited for dinner   21
6. Don't Expect much Sleep..... on overnight buses and trains   27
7. Don't Sweat about it... you can join the Chub Rub Club   35
8. Don't be Scared....you can face your fears; spiders or heights   39
9. Don't Abseil before breakfast.... you're heavier if you've eaten   49
10. Don't Wait....until you are in hospital before learning the language   53
11. Don't Get it Wet.... a zip-lock plastic bag is priceless   57
12. Don't Expose too much.... keep knickers and knockers covered   61

Summary   65

Introduction

I'm JoLo, owner/writer of the joloyolo.com blog and previously a lady of leisure. After quitting corporate work in 2015, I decided I'd join my partner and try living in Vietnam for a little while. He was out there working as a Cave Expert in the largest cave in the world and was already several steps ahead of me at living in a more remote part of the world. I was definitely out of my comfort zone, not realising that all those European holidays I'd taken each year had not quite prepared me for every eventuality I could encounter in South East Asia. I went from a city-living and loving workaholic to a fresh faced foreigner who could barely ride a bicycle and couldn't read a map. I was used to airport transfers, 18-30 holidays and girly spa breaks, not caving and trekking in the Vietnamese jungle. Life was certainly about to get more interesting for me as I tried my best to fit in to the rural location of Phong

Nha, not far from the National Park and the biggest cave in the world.

I found out through experience that you can't shit yourself on a bicycle, even with a gluten intolerance, and now I've decided that I will share with you 12 other handy travel tips, perhaps some tangible advice you can put to good use if you should ever find yourself in a similar situation. I could quite easily have written a whole book about toilet incidents but, for now, here is a mix of the things I learned most from early on in my travels. These handy travel tips are ones which I had wished I'd known before I decided to live abroad in a remote, and often humid, place where a bit of adventure was often unexpectedly on the cards.

In this short but handy travel tips book I aim to help you navigate some of the issues I faced, mainly involving embarrassing or potentially traumatic scenarios that I hope, by reading this, you can avoid – or at least laugh about afterwards! There are so many 'help' books on the market, plenty of social media posts which advise you what you should do so let's start a little bit differently; You will find 12 chapters of things not to do when on your holidays or travelling to foreign parts of the world, like Vietnam. In each chapter I will share my personal experience of that particular incident and what I should not have done at the time, to help you do it differently. Written as an eclectic mix of

'Don'ts' to help you get started and perhaps put your mind at rest of some of the concerns you may also have, as you set off to pastures new. I hope you won't need them but, if you do, I hope this list of handy travel tips will serve you well. Maybe you are already on the plane and you bought this for your journey, or you have booked your trip and already are anxious of how you will survive once in your chosen holiday destination. You could also be like I was and are just blissfully unaware of any such escapades about to come your way, that you could not even imagine needing any help or advice whatsoever. In my opinion it is better to have the information and not need it than not have it and need it, so get comfy, relax and enjoy!

Chapter 1
Don't be Shy.... of squat toilets and Bum guns

One of the first things I worry about when I'm travelling is what the toilet facilities are going to be like.

As a child I definitely used a squat in France on a family camping trip but that didn't count as I had my Mom to help me and I was nearer to the ground in height, back then.

The first time as an adult was in Vietnam, in a rural town called Phong Nha, and it most certainly wouldn't be my last. The first issue before I even got to the actual going to the toilet part is that, as an overweight forty something year old adult from England, who rarely exercised, my leg muscles were not equipped for the squatting part. Just the getting in to a squat position and back up without holding on to or touching anything was absolutely impossible for me. This was also something I did not realise until I was in the act in that Phong Nha squat toilet. I got down with just the accidental touch of an elbow on a grubby wall and I surveyed my surroundings and available apparatus as I enjoyed a long pee. Of course, I had been holding it for far too long, putting off the inevitable use of said squat toilet in unknown territory. There was a big bucket with a small tap over it and a small jug-like container with a handle, bobbing about in the water, there was no toilet paper and there was nothing within reach to hold on to. As I finished, and was expected to wash myself with the water instead of wiping with paper, I realised my legs were getting numb and I wasn't sure how to manoeuvre in to an erect position once again. Needless to say, my hands ended up touching far more toilet wall and door surfaces than I would have liked but at least I was in private.

My second attempt at the squat toilet visit was at Phong Nha cave several weeks later and had an audience. The cubicles, or lack thereof, did not have the luxury of doors or walls higher than a couple of feet. On this occasion, though, at least I got feedback and reassurance that I was doing it correctly as several Vietnamese women stared at me and checked.

After struggling to use these type of toilets I decided that exercising my legs and practicing squatting was a good idea, so I can definitely recommend that one of the best things I did was to try squatting every day, while fully clothed and in the comfort of my own home. At first holding on to a chair or table leg until I could do it unaided. A Vietnamese friend laughed at me and said the reason that they find it easier than us Westerners is because their leg muscles are longer in the calves than ours. She recommended that I now progress to squatting on a slight ramp, with my heels and back on the lower end and my toes and eyes facing up the ramp. I laughed at first but 3 minutes of this every morning, certainly worked. If only I had known any of this advice before my first experience of a squat toilet! I now still had to master the Bum gun more efficiently, though!

How Not to Use a Squat Toilet in Vietnam

1. **Ignore Your Surroundings**: Walk straight in without checking for cleanliness or available toilet paper. It's always a surprise party!
2. **Skip the Foot Placement**: Stand directly over the hole without positioning your feet properly. Why bother using the designated foot pads?
3. **Forget About Balance**: Try to squat

without holding onto anything. Who needs stability, right?
4. **Wear Complicated Clothing**: Opt for long skirts, tight pants, or anything that complicates your squatting experience. The more layers, the better!
5. **Neglect Hygiene**: Leave the toilet without washing your hands. Germs are just a natural part of life!
6. **Overlook Timing**: Spend as long as you want in there. After all, there's no line forming outside... right?
7. **Misjudge Your Aim**: Aim for the hole but miss spectacularly. Bonus points for splashes!
8. **Ignore Your Etiquette**: Leave the space as you found it - unclean and chaotic. It's a unique signature!
9. **Forget Your Supplies**: Go in without any toilet paper or wipes. Improvisation is key!
10. **Skip the Flush**: Leave everything as is and walk out without flushing. Who doesn't love a surprise for the next user?

Remember, using a squat toilet can be a unique experience! Just avoid these pitfalls, and you'll navigate it like a pro. Safe travels!

I've had many an incident with an unruly bum gun and so many friends and fellow travellers have shared with me their just as traumatic experiences so it's definitely worth preparing you for what might happen. The first thing that I was never told but wish I had been, was to be able to hold and use the apparatus with either hand. It sounds obvious but I got used to getting the right amount of water pressure, without soaking my back or legs, using my dominant hand on the trigger. I was completely taken by surprise when trying to use one in my non-dominant hand. Again, practice will help you conquer this inconvenience. There's also the surprise when the water comes directly from a roof tank which has been in the sun and is extremely hot – that can be startling! To help you navigate the toilets on your travels, do not dismiss the washlet style of toilet! While these may not leave you with an unwieldy bum gun, the water nozzle from inside the toilet can also have a mind of its own. I first encountered the washlet style toilets in Japan and found them to be most pleasant. Not only did they have the internal water pipe to wash your nether regions, but many Japanese toilets had driers, music and all sorts of settings to making doing your business, a great experience. Unfortunately, I had become complacent and also in a rush while in Malaysia. I found myself in the reception area of a large hotel chain, just before we were due to take a taxi ride to a friend's place, and I needed a quick visit to the WC facilities. My other half waited patiently for me and almost had to send in help when I didn't return for ages. In the toilet, I had merely had a quick tinkle on the overly complicated Japanese style toilet. It had a heated seat which was quite warm and with my glasses on I couldn't quite see the button to turn that off or flush. I stood up and bent over to look more closely at the many different buttons but was taken unawares when the delayed water jet popped out and blasted me forcibly in my face, knocking my glasses on to the floor and me moving backwards. I tried to push the door open, not remembering in my panic that the door was a sliding one. This resulted in my blouse becoming soaked in the water which was still shooting out from the toilet like a mini Jet d'eau in Switzerland.

On vacating the cubicle, with my glasses retrieved and my top having been under the hand-dryer to very ill effect, I had to dry the floor and my face. I actually looked like I had been in a shower fully clothed and I was still very damp when I arrived at our friends'.

If you know these types of incidents can occur, you are already more prepared for it happening than I was. Carrying a small flannel or travel towel in a plastic bag along with tissues, is a very good idea.

Here's a light-hearted list of how *not* to use a bum gun in an Asian toilet:

1. **Aimlessly Spray**: Don't just point and spray without checking your aim - this isn't a water fight!
2. **Excessive Pressure**: Avoid cranking up the pressure too high; you're not trying to create a mini water park.
3. **Neglecting the Clean-up**: Remember, don't forget to dry off afterward. Wet clothes are not a good look!
4. **Overuse**: Using it for everything is a bad idea - it's not a substitute for handwashing.
5. **Ignoring the Instructions**: If there are instructions nearby, please take a moment to read them before using it.
6. **Multitasking**: Don't try to do other things (like texting) while using the bum gun - focus is key!
7. **Squirting Without Caution**: Be mindful of your surroundings; you don't want to accidentally surprise anyone nearby.
8. **Using it as a Shower**: This is not your personal showerhead; stick to the task at hand!
9. **Forgetting the Toilet Paper**: It's often still necessary - don't dismiss the importance of a good dry!
10. **Leaving it on**: If it's a pressurised system, turning it off after use is essential; otherwise, you might have a surprise the next time someone enters!

Remember, using a bum gun can be a great experience if done correctly!

Chapter 2
Don't Take the Piss…. with a she-wee and butterflies

It probably never occurred to you that you would ever be reading about, or thinking of taking advice on, she-wees and butterflies at the same time, but allow me to explain. Firstly, I have a bit of an irrational fear of butterflies after a traumatic incident in the butterfly house at Longleat Safari park. I won't go in to that escapade, except to say that the plastic flaps on the doors are there for a reason. On my first trip in to the jungle in the Phong Nha Khe Bang National Park, with my two good friends, I thought it was a great idea to take my newly purchased she-wee. For those not familiar with this invaluable piece of equipment, it is a funnel like piece of silicone which one places at the lady's vagina in order to pee in to and aim the urine to a suitable spot on the ground or in to a bush. This saves squatting in a jungle where venomous snakes live. To get proficient at using the she-wee,

I had taken advice from other ladies and had used it while in a shower as a practice and had even got to the point where I was quite skilled with my aim.

On our trekking trip through the jungle, my friends and I needed a wee and the men folk made themselves scarce but were within earshot for any emergencies. I got out my she-wee and wrote my name in pee – granted I only have a short name, which turned out to be quite lucky. What I didn't know is that butterflies are very much attracted to urine and, within seconds, had swarmed around the steamy jet for a good drink. I was squealing like a banshee because of my irrational fear of the butterflies which made one of our male guides reappear with a machete to save me from whatever horror I had encountered in the jungle. None of us women were fully decent and some embarrassment, mainly on the guide's part, ensued.

To avoid attracting butterflies when using a she-wee, try these tips:

1. **Choose the Right Location**: Use your she-wee in areas away from flowering plants or gardens where butterflies are likely to be.
2. **Rinse and Clean**: Rinse the she-wee with water after use to minimize any lingering odours.
3. **Use Unscented Products**: Avoid any

scented wipes or products that might attract insects.
4. **Be Mindful of Timing**: Butterflies are more active during warm, sunny days. If possible, choose cooler times for your use.
5. **Cover Up**: After use, cover the area with soil or leaves if you're in a natural setting, as this can help mask any scent.

By being cautious and considerate of your surroundings, you can minimise any attraction to butterflies! You might even save a jungle guide from thinking he was about to have to capture a snake!

Chapter 3

Don't Wear…. white trousers on a cave tour

One of the most important things to consider, after booking your trip, is often what to pack and what clothing will be appropriate for whatever activities and tours you plan to do. I know as a woman of a certain age and size, it is always key for me to have bought the right clothes for my holiday, especially as I don't fit the Asian sized women's clothing.

On a few occasions, though, I have found myself falling foul of the 'all the gear but no idea' way of doing things as well as being the least adequately equipped on a group tour. One particular time I was so pleased with my packing and had got it down to a fine art. My travel bag contained minimal shoes, the right amount of underwear and just enough tops and bottoms which could be mixed and matched. My partner, two friends and I had booked to go on a two day cave and jungle trek in Vietnam and I thought I had packed suitably. I turned up to day one wearing good footwear with grip; Innovate fell running shoes, I had a lightweight top and over shirt and some lightweight white trousers, which could be rolled up to make shorts. You may already be one step ahead of me, or you may be thinking as I did, that white trousers would be a great idea for a jungle trek. What I did not take in to account was the humidity, the dirt, the plants, the river crossings, the sweat, blood and (probably) tears that I would encounter within a few minutes of setting off. I had definitely not planned to go sliding down a steep hill on my bum and ending up looking like I had soiled myself! If that wasn't bad enough, after an attempt to wash the mud and plant stains from my white trousers, my friends noticed that they were see-through as I wandered in the sunlight at the front of the group trying to dry off. They did not dry as the humidity was high and then we were in a cave shortly after where I would remain for the rest of the day - in wet and muddy, almost transparent, white trousers! I do not recommend it.

Here's a list of more sensible reasons not to wear white trousers while in a cave or on a jungle trek:

1. **Stains and Dirt**: White trousers easily

show mud, dirt, and stains, making them look dirty quickly.
2. **Limited Camouflage**: In jungle environments, white stands out, making you more visible to insects and wildlife.
3. **Wet Conditions**: Caves and jungles often have moisture; white fabric shows wet spots and can become see-through when damp.
4. **Comfort and Flexibility**: White trousers may not be made of materials suitable for rugged activities, limiting movement.
5. **Heat Absorption**: In a jungle, white might reflect sunlight, but it can also lead to sunburn if you're exposed for long periods.
6. **Care Requirements**: White clothing often requires special care to maintain its brightness, which is impractical in remote areas.
7. **Insect Attraction**: Lighter colours can attract more insects, increasing the chance of bites and stings.
8. **Risk of Damage**: Scratches and tears are more noticeable on white fabric, making it seem worn out more quickly.
9. **Distraction**: Bright white can draw attention to you in a wildlife setting, potentially disturbing local fauna.
10. **Less Breathable Options**: Many white

trousers may be made from non-breathable fabrics that trap heat and moisture.

These reasons can help you decide on more practical clothing choices for your adventure!

Chapter 4
Don't Run another Man's Race...when you can't even jog

One of the best pieces of advice I have ever had was to 'never run another man's race' and I didn't appreciate at the time just how priceless this would be for the rest of my life. It was the first time I had heard the phrase while on a jungle trek that I had been talked in to over a drink with two friends. I'd drunkenly agreed to do the 4 day Tu Lan Expedition with Oxalis Adventure Tours in Phong Nha, Vietnam, during July, when it was so hot and humid. I was unfit and probably should not have undertaken such a difficult and lengthy adventure tour without more experience, however, as my other half worked for the company, I didn't want to embarrass myself or him. On day one of the trek I was struggling and one of the other guests, Tan, was helping me pace myself. I kept on thinking I had to keep up with the group and I was comparing myself all the time with others and their achievements. Even the guide had already told me that if I wasn't up to it, he had no qualms about turning me back so I was concerned I wasn't good enough. There were all sorts of people on the group and all had different physical strengths, Tan, being one of the strong guys and extremely fit. Tan had explained that I should choose my own pace and let my own mind decide when I needed a rest. He said I would know if I was someone who could plod on slowly but keep going or if I was the type of person who could go more quickly for a shorter burst before taking a rest. Was I better on the uphill or the downhill and di I prefer to admire the view points with my eyes rather than my camera? Tan was wise and I eventually figured out what his advice meant to me and realised that mental strength of a person doing something physical is just as important. I decided that I was not going to let the self-doubts get to me and, when I knew something was really out of my capabilities, I would hold no shame in saying so. Needless to say, I ended up sitting out the third day at the Tu Lan Head Office while the rest of my group walked up and over a mountain, in blistering hot sun. I still had to be taken on the back of a porter's motorbike to get to the resting spot and then got picked back up to walk through the jungle to the Day 3 campsite so it wasn't just a walk in the park. That evening, I was thankful that I had missed the gruelling walk as my trip buddies were aching and sunburned despite the amount of sun cream they had applied.

From that point on, I have always thought of Tan when I've found myself in a situation where I may have previously tried to 'keep up' with someone who was not a match, physically. As I have got older I'm also so much more aware of when to push myself and when to sit it out.

Running another person's race can lead to a few pitfalls. Here are some reasons to avoid it:

1. **Individual Goals**: Everyone has their own aspirations and motivations. Focusing on someone else's journey can distract you from your own goals.
2. **Different Circumstances**: Each person faces unique challenges and advantages. What works for one might not work for another, leading to frustration or burnout.
3. **Self-Discovery**: Personal growth comes from navigating your own experiences. Embracing your path allows you to learn and evolve in ways that mimic someone else's journey can't.
4. **Authenticity**: Authenticity fosters genuine connections. When you run your own race, you're more likely to attract like-minded individuals who resonate with your true self.

5. **Comparison Trap**: Constantly measuring yourself against others can erode your self-esteem and motivation. It's healthier to focus on your own progress and celebrate your unique achievements.

By prioritising your own race, you can cultivate a fulfilling journey that's genuinely yours! Alternatively you can just adjust your mind-set so that you really don't care about the other customers' stamina on your shared group tour. As I've got older I've applied this rule to many events and tours and I have certainly enjoyed them a lot more than trying to keep up with the fittest in the group.

Chapter 5
Don't Swallow it All....
especially when invited for dinner

Whenever I am away from home and staying abroad for any length of time, I have been lucky enough to make local friends who have invited me to parties, weddings and meals at their homes. In South East Asia it is very rare to meet a local with a food allergy, or at least one who knows they have one. I, on the other hand, have often found myself in compromised or embarrassing situations as I do have food allergies but am also quite fussy with what I like to eat. Family and close friends would probably confirm that it would be easier for me to make a list of food I do like to eat, rather than list the foods I try to avoid. When I first went to a local eatery in Phong Nha, Vietnam, I was surprised how much the locals liked the parts of the animal we would normally, in the Western world, never touch. I for one have never crunched on a chicken bone or eaten the neck or bum of any animal (well, knowingly)!

On many a Tet holiday or wedding related celebration I have been known to take a piece of meat from the offerings to find I had mistakenly chosen the neck or bum. In fact my other half thinks I have a knack for seeking it out! Unfortunately, once you have it in your mouth and have realised which part you have, it is too late. It doesn't help to know that your fellow diners may often be looking at you expectantly, as you're the new person, and they want to check that you like the food and are waiting for you to swallow it so they can force another piece in to your bowl. My top tip is to have some tissues in your pocket so you can politely get rid of it – otherwise all the nice bits will have been eaten by the time you've chewed through that one tough bit. As the locals got to know me a little better they were much more receptive to my allergies and I was able to feel confident enough to say I didn't eat something I felt I couldn't.

It is also common for the local people to want to share some of their fanciest dishes in order to thank or impress you. After numerous visits to a physiotherapist in Dong Hoi, I became good friends with my therapist and owner of the practice, Thuy. One of my most memorable Vietnamese food experiences was when Thuy invited my other half and I to a special restaurant in Dong Hoi and I was so underprepared for what was about to unfold.

Five adults and 2 children squeezed in to one taxi and we drove out in to the middle of nowhere, stopping at an empty café, with plastic chairs. Thuy took the liberty of ordering for us and, from what we could make out, we were getting an assortment of bird dishes, grilled or fried and some cooked with bamboo. Fried rice was ordered, kimchi on the table already, a case of beers and a bucket of ice. I should have realised it was going to be challenging for me, when all the Vietnamese adults got straight on the beers!! More diners began to arrive and most of them had big families so I started to feel a bit more relaxed that all would be fine, the place was clean and well run. The first dish to come out was a bowl of about 20 or so small birds which were sparrows and they were to be eaten whole, the bones the heads, the feet - the whole shebang! I felt sick already but actually the sparrows tasted pretty good, although I couldn't bring myself to eat the head and bones so I picked at it like it was a miniature Kentucky Fried Chicken. I managed 4 sparrows but my partner really did take one for the team on that plate. The next dish to come to the table was the fried rice which I heartily filled my bowl up with, not realising it had minced bird in it as an ingredient! It tasted bad but I managed to smile and force it down, encouraging fellow diners to have more. Everyone else was really enjoying it and I was drinking quite a lot of beer to wash my food down, despite my gluten allergy at that time. The second bird dish to come out was described as kingfisher but it was actually an egret, it tasted like the smell of a fishy wet dog! I had one piece and was willing myself not to be sick!! The third dish I had no idea what the bird was, but it was served with sautéed bamboo, which neither of us liked. I thought it might be the least offensive ingredient in the pot and I decided to pull the 'I'm full' card, fearing the worst. Over a week later I found out it was boiled white duck, which I would probably have enjoyed the most out of the whole dining experience. Finally, we were done and I didn't dare think about what we had just eaten or I would be sick. I was very grateful to our hosts for them to have thought about us so I didn't want to offend by not enjoying the food – I did need a bathroom, though!

Here are some reasons to avoid eating the bum or neck of a cooked bird:

1. **Texture**: The bum (or butt) and neck tend to have a different texture than the meatier parts, which may not be as appealing to some.
2. **Flavour**: These parts can have a stronger,

gamier flavour that might not be enjoyable for everyone.

3. **Fat Content**: The bum often contains more fat, which can be greasy and unappetising.
4. **Hygiene Concerns**: The bum is near the digestive tract, so there may be a higher risk of bacteria or contaminants.
5. **Bones**: The neck contains more small bones, which can be a choking hazard and make it difficult to eat.
6. **Presentation**: In many cultures, the bum and neck are not considered desirable cuts, which might affect the overall appeal of a dish.
7. **Personal Preference**: Many people simply prefer to eat the more traditional cuts of meat, such as the breast and thighs.
8. **Culinary Traditions**: In some cuisines, these parts are often used for stock or broth rather than served as main dishes.

If you're considering them for cooking, they can still be used effectively in stocks or soups! By all means, try all the food you are offered and make up your own mind, but use these experiences to guide you if you get in bit of a jam.

Chapter 6
Don't Expect much Sleep..... on overnight buses and trains

It is worth stating that I am a really bad traveller, even as a child I would get travel sick going by car to visit my grandparents, who lived in the same town! Before any long journey I always get a little nervous as I know that the likelihood of me needing the toilet is going to be very high. There has been numerous times where I have not been able to get on a bus tour, or even had to get off in an emergency situation. For that reason, as well as safety and comfort, I much prefer to take the train. This is especially true when I am in Vietnam and I actually quite enjoy a sleeper bunk on a train.

I wish I had known before a train journey that there are alternate types of toilet at each end of the carriage; squat and western style. I always found myself in squat toilets and had no idea that the other one was a western style so I struggled to squat on a moving train. The toilets are also not always up to the cleanliness you might expect but they aren't the worst I've ever been to. There is a café carriage which usually sells snacks, soft drinks and beers which are very reasonably priced but depending on the time of your train they may run out of your preferences. I recommend taking snacks and water on with you so that you don't have to bother with the café carriage.

Also be prepared that the temperature could get stuck at cold Air Con or not work at all and it be sweaty so make sure you have the right clothes for any possible temperature.

In Vietnamese culture, parents and grandparents will not shush their children and my worst train journey was where Grandma had given a toddler a whistle – 8 hours of that was too much for anyone to put up with! If you have a bottom bunk be prepared for other people in your, or even a nearby, compartment to want to share it. I always book the top bunk if I can but this is also worthy of some tips.

Make sure if you book the top bunk that you are able to climb up and down as it isn't for someone with a leg injury. Also be prepared for the bunks to be pretty firm, as most beds and seats are in Vietnam.

If a sleeper is not available or you are going a shorter journey, the soft seats are pretty comfy as long as you are not overly tall - they do recline for a bit of a snooze. Do keep in mind that if it is daylight outside then the locals will be awake and noisy, no one wears head phones and there will be so many people having loud telephone conversations that you will wonder what they are finding to talk about for so long.

My last top tip for train travel is to set an alarm for 10 minutes before you are due to arrive at your destination so that you don't miss your stop.

Travelling by train in Vietnam can be a wonderful experience, but there are some key "do nots" to keep in mind for a smooth journey:

Do Nots of Train Travel

1. **Do Not Arrive Late**: Train schedules can be strict. Arriving at the station early helps avoid any last-minute stress.
2. **Do Not Forget Your ID**: Always carry your passport or ID, as you'll need it for ticket checks – you will need to show your ticket as you get on to the train, as well as a check from the inspector when on the train.
3. **Do Not Bring Excessive Luggage**: Space can be limited, especially in sleeper cars. Stick to a manageable amount of luggage.

4. **Do Not Ignore Local Etiquette**: Be respectful of local customs, like being quiet during night travel and giving up your seat to the elderly or families.
5. **Do Not Eat Strong-Smelling Food**: While snacks are welcome, avoid bringing food with strong odours that might disturb fellow passengers. Durian fruit is banned on public transport because of the strong smell.
6. **Do Not Rely Solely on English**: While many staff speak some English, it's helpful to learn basic phrases for smoother communication.
7. **Do Not Leave Valuables Unattended**: Keep your belongings secure and within sight, especially during stops.
8. **Do Not Disrespect Train Staff**: Train personnel are there to help. Politeness goes a long way.
9. **Do Not Forget to Use the Restroom before Departure**: Facilities can be limited, especially on longer journeys.
10. **Do Not Expect Wi-Fi Everywhere**: Connectivity can be spotty or non-existent; download any necessary information or entertainment beforehand.

By keeping these tips in mind, you can ensure a

more enjoyable train journey through the beautiful landscapes of Vietnam!

You may decide to travel by another mode. Traveling by sleeper bus can be a unique experience, but there are definitely some do's and don'ts to keep in mind for a smoother journey. Here are some key "do nots":

Do Nots of Sleeper Bus Travel

1. **Don't Over pack**: Sleeper buses have limited space, so avoid bringing large luggage. Stick to a small backpack or suitcase.
2. **Don't Ignore Local Customs**: Be respectful of local customs, such as removing your shoes before entering the bus.
3. **Don't Expect a Private Experience**: Sleeper buses can be crowded. Be prepared to share your space with fellow travellers.
4. **Don't Sit Up Too Early**: If you're in the lower bunk, avoid sitting up quickly as it might be cramped and uncomfortable.
5. **Don't Forget Snacks and Water**: While some buses offer snacks, it's wise to bring your own, as well as a water bottle.
6. **Don't Distract the Driver**: Keep noise

levels down and avoid talking to the driver to ensure everyone's safety.
7. **Don't Leave Valuables Unattended**: Always keep an eye on your belongings and avoid leaving valuables in the overhead compartments.
8. **Don't Rely on Wi-Fi**: Not all sleeper buses provide Wi-Fi, so plan accordingly and download any necessary content beforehand.
9. **Don't Be Late**: Arrive at the bus station on time. Buses often leave promptly, and you don't want to miss your ride.
10. **Don't Overlook Personal Comfort**: Bring a neck pillow, blanket, or travel essentials to make your journey more comfortable. Hand sanitiser is a good idea.

Following these tips can help you enjoy your sleeper bus experience!

Depending on where you are from in the world and what level of transport safety you have come to expect, will have a massive bearing on whether you can tolerate the sleeper buses or not. If, like me, you are blissfully unaware of the accident rates then I recommend you remain that way while travelling on long distance buses in Vietnam. I have heard so many horror stories but my partner and I have never had any crazy experiences in over 10 years of being there, thankfully. I have noticed that if you are a Westerner then the driver will do everything they can to make you go to the back of the bus. I've noticed in Vietnam that the locals don't seem to travel well and are often travel sick which is one of the reasons the driver wants to put them at the front. The sleeper buses often have 3 rows across and 2 bunks which also mean that us Westerners are made to go on the upper decks, the middle and the furthest back. On one journey with an over 70 year old Australian friend, the driver got so mad with us for not obeying his wishes that he slapped us with his clipboard so be prepared to do as you're told. On another journey a young girl who was only 3 rows from the front puked what looked like sticky rice all over the bus and seats. Even before Covid, all the local passengers wear a mask and I would definitely recommend doing that. My longest journey on one of those buses was actually during the day time and was to go to the Laos boarder and back in a day. The journey was 15 hours long and was actually not that bad. Be warned, though, you will only be able to go to the toilet when they stop for petrol/gas as there are not toilets on most of the buses. If you are similar to me and have a sensitive stomach I would recommend taking your own snacks and dry crackers plus hand sanitiser as most service stops have a distinct lack of soap and limited food options for people with allergies. In the past I have taken travel sickness pills and some of them have knocked me out which has been really helpful, but of course you should check they suit you before relying on any medication.

Chapter 7
Don't Sweat about it... you can join the Chub Rub Club

I'm a woman of a certain age and have been mildly to fully overweight for a good portion of my adult life so I'm sure no one is shocked to read that I have suffered with what I like to call Chub Rub. For those of you fortunate to have avoided this affliction it is usually where, due to being overweight and/or sweaty, your skin on two or more body parts rubs and causes soreness. Let me give you more of an example; when not wearing trousers or longer shorts my thighs will rub together as I walk, stick together as I stand and generally get sore from being sweaty in the humidity of South East Asia. This can very quickly become very unpleasant and often prevent walking for longer/further during your sightseeing trips. It can also be an issue for the bigger-boobed ladies and can even cause an under boob rash which can be irritated by bras. To prevent myself from getting

Chub Rub I will always wear cycling shorts under a skirt or dress where possible, if that isn't possible then I will use a non-perfumed, non-whitening stick deodorant applied on the thighs (and the underboob) before I get dressed. This will increase the amount of time you have before the Chub Rub kicks in, but is not a fool proof method. I would recommend taking talcum powder with you so that you can dust it on places that might need a bit of help to not rub together, but be warned that it can go a bit clumpy if the humidity is too high.

Preventing chafing of the thighs can make a big difference while on a holiday, in comfort during walks or workouts. Here are some helpful hints for you to try, to prevent the annoying discomfort.

1. **Wear the Right Clothing**: Opt for moisture-wicking, breathable fabrics that fit well. Avoid cotton, which retains moisture.
2. **Choose the Right Fit**: Look for shorts or leggings that are snug but not too tight. Longer styles can provide more coverage.
3. **Use Anti-Chafing Products**: Consider applying anti-chafing creams, balms, or powders to reduce friction. Look for products designed specifically for this purpose.
4. **Stay Dry**: Keep your skin dry by using body powder in areas prone to chafing. Changing

into dry clothes after sweating can also help.

5. **Hydrate and Moisturise**: Keeping your skin well-hydrated can improve its elasticity and resilience. Use a good moisturiser regularly.
6. **Take Breaks**: If you're walking or exercising for long periods, take breaks to allow your skin to breathe and reduce friction.
7. **Shave or Trim Hair**: For some, reducing hair in the chafing area can help minimize friction.
8. **Consider Compression Garments**: Compression shorts can provide support and reduce rubbing between the thighs.
9. **Stay Aware of Your Movements**: Be mindful of your walking or running form to minimize thigh contact.
10. **Test Your Gear**: Before a long walk or workout, try out your clothing and products to see what works best for you.

Implementing these tips can help keep you comfortable and chafe-free during your activities!

Chapter 8

Don't be Scared....you can face your fears; spiders or heights

I think most people have irrational fears and often this doesn't cause much of a problem in everyday life. I never needed to avoid heights or massive spiders when I worked in an office in Sheffield! After moving to Vietnam and travelling around places in South East Asia and Australia, these types of fears became more restricting for me and I had to deal with them. It didn't help that my other half is not scared of anything and really didn't understand what I was so worried about. Since being a child, I had always been scared of spiders and my Mom had to catch them and move them for me. Even in adulthood, I once stayed at a friend's when there was a spider in my house which I couldn't get to. Before I went to live in Phong Nha I didn't know I was scared of heights as I had never had to go any higher than the ladder of a bunk bed or a spiral staircase in someone's home. I also didn't know if I was scared of snakes as I had only ever held one at a zoo as a young kid. I'd only become scared of butterflies as an adult after an 'attack' in a butterfly house. Since living abroad, I definitely had to reassess my fears (irrational or not) and a few incidents sprung to mind which might help you, as fellow travellers, to overcome yours. On a caving expedition we were in quite a small cave but big enough that it wasn't claustrophobic at all. It was called Secret Cave and it had a secret exit at the back of the cave which had two things that I was scared of, at the same time. There was a bit of a squeeze through where I had already torn my top when I got a boob stuck on a stalactite (not a known fear so I was ok), before I had to abseil down quite a drop while being watched. Above our heads were spiders as big as dinner plates with grey eyes! At first I thought they were drawings on the cave ceiling, until I saw one of their eyes move. I did not know what to complain about first; the spiders or the height I was possibly about to fall off, in to deep water. It turned out that after getting more information about the spiders, although big, rarely moving and not being dangerous, my body was more worried about falling off a height. It took me a while and I was attached to a rope, but when I ended up, upside down and squealing like a banshee, I knew I was more scared of the abseil. It did not help that I was meant to be able to complete the abseil successfully on to a raft which was bobbing about in an underground lake – something I never knew I had to be scared of, but wish I had.

Another time I was in a cave when the tour guide told me to jump across the rock I was on to the one he was on. I am not made for jumping across rocks in a dark cave so I stood still and asked why. The guide, somewhat panicked said there was a snake on my rock but I couldn't see it and asked him where. This was great as it proved to me that I was less scared by a snake than my guide seemed to be and when I did see it, it was only small and possibly a viper but I stayed really calm, grabbed the guides hand and got off my rock.

I've since had two other experiences with snakes, both in Vietnam and both were cobras and, I was not scared. One was an adult cobra which slithered across the tarpaulin in the clearing we had picked for our picnic and the other was in the street where I was riding my bicycle – both were not wanting to hurt a person and were just looking for food and a quick exit.

While I was in Australia I was waiting by the entrance to a cave and chatting to a guy who had turned up late and missed the tour that was happening in the cave. We were sat next to a wall and there was a Red Back next to my shoulder, which I didn't realise until this chap told me to move forward a bit. I was a bit freaked out but not quite as bad as I had been previously – maybe I was finally overcoming my fear of spiders.

Choosing which fear is scarier between heights and spiders can be subjective and depends on personal experiences and feelings. Here are some factors to consider, like I did:

1. **Physical Reaction**: Pay attention to which fear causes a stronger physical response - like increased heart rate, sweating, or dizziness.
2. **Impact on Daily Life**: Consider how each fear affects your daily activities. Does fear of heights limit your ability to go certain places, or does fear of spiders make you anxious in your home?
3. **Control**: Think about how much control you feel over each situation. For example, can you avoid heights more easily than you can avoid spiders?
4. **Duration and Intensity**: Reflect on which fear lingers longer in your mind or causes more intense anxiety.
5. **Past Experiences**: Consider any past experiences you've had with either fear. Traumatic incidents can heighten the fear associated with them.

6. **Cultural Influences**: Sometimes, societal or cultural narratives can influence which fears seem scarier.

Ultimately, it's a personal decision, and what's most frightening to one person may not be to another.

Encountering a spider in Vietnam, or anywhere, can be unsettling! Here are some "do nots" to keep in mind:

1. **Don't Panic**: Staying calm can help you assess the situation better. Panicking may lead to rash actions.
2. **Don't Swat at It**: Swatting can provoke the spider, making it more likely to bite or escape in a way that might lead to more anxiety.
3. **Don't Get Too Close**: Maintain a safe distance. Most spiders are harmless, but it's best to avoid direct contact.
4. **Don't Assume It's Dangerous**: Not all spiders are venomous. Take a moment to identify it if you can, or just give it space.
5. **Don't Leave Food Exposed**: If you're in a living area, avoid leaving food out, which can attract spiders.
6. **Don't Touch It**: Unless you're sure about what you're dealing with, avoid touching the spider.

7. **Don't Ignore It If You're Uncomfortable**: If the spider is in your living space and it's making you uncomfortable, consider relocating it (safely) or seeking help.
8. **Don't Forget to Check Your Shoes or Clothes**: Especially in tropical climates, spiders can hide in clothing or shoes, so always check them before putting them on.

Staying composed and taking sensible actions can help you deal with the situation effectively!

When dealing with a fear of heights in a jungle or cave, here are some important "do nots" to keep in mind:

Do Nots

1. **Do Not Rush**: Avoid hurrying through areas that trigger your fear. Take your time to acclimate to the environment.
2. **Do Not Look Down**: If you're on a ledge or high ground, try not to look down. Focus on the horizon or something stable ahead of you.
3. **Do Not Go Alone**: Avoid exploring high or precarious areas by yourself. Having a companion can provide support and safety.
4. **Do Not Force Yourself**: Don't push yourself to confront your fear if you're not ready. It's okay to take a step back.

5. **Do Not Ignore Your Feelings**: If you feel overwhelmed, acknowledge your fear instead of trying to suppress it. It's okay to feel scared.
6. **Do Not Engage in Risky Behaviour**: Avoid taking unnecessary risks, such as climbing unstable rocks or moving too close to ledges. That Instagram photo is definitely not worth getting an injury for.
7. **Do Not Avoid Grounded Areas Completely**: While it's good to be cautious, don't completely avoid heights. Gradually exposing yourself to safe elevated areas can help.
8. **Do Not Forget to Breathe**: If you start to feel anxious, don't forget to breathe deeply and steadily. This can help calm your mind.
9. **Do Not Dismiss Preparation**: Avoid going into challenging areas without proper preparation, equipment, or guidance. Make sure you're equipped to handle the environment.
10. **Do Not Compare Yourself to Others**: Everyone has different comfort levels with heights. Focus on your own progress rather than how others handle similar situations.

Tips for Managing Fear

- **Grounding Techniques**: Use techniques like visualisation or focusing on your breath to help manage anxiety.
- **Practice Gradually**: Start with low heights and gradually work your way up as you build confidence.
- **Seek Professional Help**: If your fear is severe, consider talking to a therapist who specialises in phobias.

Taking it slow and being mindful of your limits can help you navigate your fear in these environments. Failing that, wear good underwear!!

When landing on a raft in water, it's important to prioritise safety. Here are some things to avoid:

1. **Jumping or Leaping**: Avoid jumping onto the raft, as this can destabilise it and cause it to tip over or move.
2. **Rushing**: Don't hurry onto the raft; take your time to ensure you're balanced and steady.
3. **Carrying Heavy Items**: Avoid carrying heavy gear or equipment when boarding, as this can affect your balance and make it harder to stabilise the raft.

4. **Ignoring Stability**: Don't disregard the raft's movement; be aware of the waves and the raft's position before stepping on.
5. **Disregarding Instructions**: If there are specific instructions from the raft's crew or tour guides, don't ignore them.
6. **Overloading**: Avoid overloading the raft with too many people or equipment, as this increases the risk of capsizing.
7. **Standing Up Immediately**: Once on the raft, avoid moving about if you can. Wait until everyone is settled and the raft is stable.
8. **Not Assessing Conditions**: Don't neglect to assess weather and water conditions before boarding; strong winds or currents can affect safety.

By keeping these tips in mind, you can help ensure a safer experience when landing on a raft or similar.

Chapter 9

Don't Abseil before breakfast.... you're heavier if you've eaten

Abseiling on an empty stomach can be risky for several reasons:

1. **Energy Levels**: Abseiling requires physical effort and focus. Without food, you may lack the energy needed to perform safely and effectively.
2. **Concentration**: Low blood sugar can impair your concentration and decision-making, increasing the risk of accidents.
3. **Fatigue**: Physical activities can be tiring, and if you haven't eaten, you might fatigue more quickly, making you less responsive to challenges.
4. **Dizziness or Nausea**: Exercising on an empty stomach can lead to dizziness or nausea, which could be dangerous when you're in a precarious position.

5. **Overall Performance**: Proper nutrition helps with endurance and strength, which are crucial for safe abseiling.

It's best to have a light snack or meal before heading out to ensure you're physically and mentally prepared. Of course, on my first ever attempt at an abseil, I had taken none of this advice in to consideration as I didn't know. All I had been told was that I was going to be abseiling off the roof of our four story house and that I could go for breakfast as soon as I had done it. My other half came up the stairs with ropes and some harnesses and said to follow him. It sounded simple to the people who were there, who all had abseiled numerous times. Just looking over the edge was enough to create panic in my head as I got clipped in to a harness for the first time and put on some specific gloves with grips on. I was listening to all the instructions but I knew they would leave my mind once I got started. It took my partner, who was in charge of the operation, ages to convince me to do it as I wouldn't climb over the balcony or roof wall and hold on to the other side of the building, despite being 'clipped on'. I was shaking like a shitting dog as I got in to position and I actually could have cried from fear. We had more people at the top trying to talk me in to abseiling down than we had at the bottom to catch me if/when it went wrong. The previous evening I had seen a video clip of a window cleaner being blown off a skyscraper and smacking in to the side of the building so I didn't have much faith in my own abilities.

It took so long that I didn't know if I was passing out from hunger, fear or a good mixture of both. I definitely should have been better prepared and maybe even have done a bit of research. The first time I did it I couldn't squeeze the descender hard enough with my left hand so I got stuck at my balcony for a short time which worried me. Once I did get going, I was scared the whole way down and I really wished I had been wearing better underwear! The 'elephant pant' style trousers I was sporting were definitely not helpful in any way.

Chapter 10
Don't Wait....until you are in hospital before learning the language

This is the chapter that I almost didn't include and hope that none of you need to have read it but if it helps just one person from something pretty dangerous, then it will have been worth it. To give a bit of context, my partner can speak a bit of Vietnamese and I had had some lessons but I am unable to speak much that can be understood. I had also been in Vietnam throughout Covid and we lived in the small town of Phong Nha. We were 50km away from the nearest hospital and had not been able to leave our village due to the lockdown restrictions. After one particular lock down, we were allowed back out to the bars and restaurants that had opened and I was so excited to head out for food and drinks that I forgot to take off my flip-flops that I wore around the house. I ended up slipping on a wet floor in the cheap flip-flops and hurt my leg, resulting in me being unable to walk at all. A good friend had to take me home on the back of a motorbike, in the dark, and I had to be carried up two flights of stairs and put in to bed, in agony. It wasn't for another week that we were able to go to the nearest city and see a doctor at the hospital in Dong Hoi. The doctor spoke English and referred me for an MRI later that day which I was impressed with the speed of the appointment. I went back, with my partner and a work colleague of his in case we needed anything translating. What then happened was rather embarrassing and worrying, all because I didn't have the ability to speak to the MRI technician in Vietnamese. I was already in situ, awaiting the start of the MRI scan, when I realised they had not asked me to remove any jewellery. which I understand they usually do in the UK. I have a piercing in an intimate place and I needed to check if it needed to be removed. I ended up having to tell my partner who had to ask his male work colleague to come in to the room to translate this question to the technician for us and it was all very embarrassing for all the men involved. It was made worse that it wasn't necessary to be removed for my MRI scan but I was still quite certain that the broken conversation and pointing at my body were still less embarrassing than anyone having to scrape my undercarriage from the inside of a magnetic tube! So, learn from my lucky escape and learn a bit of the language of the country you're going to, make sure you have Google Translate on your phone and potentially use some or all of this advice, should you be unfortunate enough to have to need it;

When having an MRI in a foreign hospital, it's important to communicate effectively and respectfully. Here are some things to avoid:

1. **Assuming Language Proficiency**: Don't assume everyone speaks your language fluently. Use simple words or gestures if needed, and be patient.
2. **Making Jokes about the Procedure**: Humour can be misunderstood, especially in a medical context. Keep the atmosphere professional and respectful.
3. **Ignoring Instructions**: If staff give you specific instructions, follow them closely. Don't hesitate to ask for clarification if you're unsure.
4. **Being Impatient**: Medical facilities can have different processes. Be patient with the staff and the waiting times.
5. **Discussing Personal Health Issues Too Freely**: While you might feel comfortable, be aware of cultural differences regarding privacy and medical discussions.
6. **Forgetting to Communicate Concerns**: If you have anxiety about the procedure or any medical conditions, express these

concerns rather than keeping them to yourself.

7. **Using Technical Terms**: If you're discussing your medical history, avoid using complex medical jargon that may not translate well.
8. **Disregarding Cultural Norms**: Familiarise yourself with local customs and etiquette. What's acceptable in one culture may not be in another.
9. **Bringing Unnecessary Items**: Avoid bringing items that are not allowed in the MRI room, such as metal objects, unless you confirm its okay.
10. **Neglecting to Follow Up**: After the procedure, ensure you understand how and when to receive your results, especially if you have a language barrier.

Overall, approach the situation with respect and open communication as much as you can and be sure to get the best Insurance you can.

Chapter 11

Don't Get it Wet.... a zip-lock plastic bag is priceless

This handy travel tip is so obvious that you'd think that we would all know and do this already, however, you would be surprised! I've lost count of how many people I have seen in Asia shoving their gadgets in to a bag of rice in a desperate attempt to save a phone that has been soaked in a monsoon rain. There will be times where you think there is just no chance of rain or your phone getting wet while you are enjoying a spot of travelling. For the sake of making sure you have some intact Ziploc bags, you can protect any valuable items that will need it. Nowadays, my passport lives in a Ziploc bag. If I need a visa to enter a country, I print it out and put it in a Ziploc bag. When I pack my hand luggage I also print out my travel insurance document, put it in a Ziploc bag and store it in the inside zip pocket of the case/backpack. When leaving the airport or walking between my hotel and a restaurant, shop or bar I will put my phone in a, you guessed it, Ziploc bag. This will protect your belongings and can be used for all sorts of things whilst travelling.

A Ziploc bag is a solo traveller's best friend for several reasons:

1. **Organisation**: It helps keep your items organised, whether it's toiletries, snacks, or small electronics. You can easily see what's inside without rummaging through your bag.
2. **Protection**: It protects items from moisture and spills, which is especially useful for toiletries or food. If something leaks, it won't ruin your other belongings.
3. **Space-saving**: You can compress items, like clothes or snacks, making packing more efficient.
4. **Versatility**: Use it for a variety of purposes: storing documents, separating dirty laundry, or even as a makeshift ice pack.
5. **Convenience**: Easy to pack and access, making it great for day trips or outings where you need quick access to snacks or essentials.

Overall, it's a simple, lightweight, and multifunctional item that can really enhance your travel experience! If you're travelling to an area with a likelihood of monsoon rains and sporadic downpours, I would also recommend taking a large plastic bag which will fit in your luggage as a liner, you can tie it up and prevent your entire belongings from getting wet.

Chapter 12

Don't Expose too much.... keep knickers and knockers covered

This handy tip is really obvious and even people who aren't travel savvy will have at least googled what not to do/wear in the country they are planning to visit, I'm sure, but one of my funniest memories in Vietnam is about this topic. I was helping out with English practice with staff in a café which had a convenience store type shelf selling useful essentials. Most of the staff were young Vietnamese girls but there were 2 Vietnamese guys who also worked there, one of who was only 18 and quite shy and innocent. The café was located centrally and next door to a backpacker hostel so there was plenty of customers for food and drink. A young English girl came in to buy something off the shelf in the shop and was wearing a skimpy beige bikini and flip-flops. I did a double take as, at first glance, she actually looked like she was naked from a distance. Some of the female staff were giggling from embarrassment and I decided I would go over to the customer and ask her to put some clothes on, or a towel around her at the very least. As I was crossing the room, the young male member of staff caught sight of the customer and could not hide his shock. He was rooted to the spot, his face was bright red and he did not know what to do. I felt so sorry for him as all the other staff noticed and started to laugh and point. This was all very innocent however it made me realise how the culture of covering up in other countries means that there is often so much shock and embarrassment for the locals. It also made me feel a bit responsible that people from my own country could make someone feel so out of sorts by not thinking about this cultural difference.

Some people may be of the mind that it is hot so the less clothes the better but then I started to notice bikini clad girls on motorbikes and that really did upset me. The scars from the gravel rash alone can be pretty horrendous should even the smallest of accidents occur, so I would definitely urge you to cover up appropriately when in a foreign land – and that's not just because I'm old and overweight! It will keep you safe. In the sunny months the UV is very high in a lot of places and sun cream can start to sweat or rub off – popping a cover up or a T-shirt and shorts/trousers on that are a decent length, can be a good idea.

When visiting other countries, it's important to be mindful of local customs and cultural norms regarding clothing. Here are some guidelines on when not to wear inappropriate clothing, including bikinis:

1. **Religious Sites**: When visiting temples, pagodas, and other religious sites, it's essential to dress modestly. This usually means covering your shoulders and knees. Avoid wearing bikinis or revealing outfits in these areas. No one needs to see any religion revealing parts of your body.
2. **Rural Areas**: In more rural or traditional areas, people tend to dress conservatively. It's respectful to wear clothing that covers your arms and legs.
3. **Markets and Local Areas**: While you might see tourists in casual attire, it's a good idea to avoid overly revealing clothing in local markets or when interacting with residents.
4. **Public Transport**: On public transport, especially buses or trains, wearing modest clothing is advisable to respect local customs and avoid drawing unnecessary attention.
5. **Restaurants and Cafés**: Upscale dining establishments may have dress codes. In

general, it's best to avoid swimwear unless you're at a beach resort.
6. **Beach Etiquette**: While it's acceptable to wear bikinis on the beach, it's best to cover up with a sarong or dress when leaving the beach area, especially when walking through local towns or markets.
7. **Nightlife**: In nightlife areas, you can be a bit more relaxed, but still aim for stylish, casual attire rather than swimwear.

Overall, when in doubt, opt for clothing that covers more skin and reflects the local culture. It shows respect and helps you blend in better with the local community. Lots of garments can be purchased while away but I found that it's very tricky to buy a good fitting bra when you're not in a country that has bigger women.

Summary

You've now had a glimpse in to my world and, hopefully, read some handy travel advice and tips to help you get started on your travels. Whether it be a solo trip to Asia or finding yourself in a remote part of the world with different ways to your own country's, let this give you some reassurance that anything can happen but you can deal with it and survive, like I did.

So, 'You Can't Shit Yourself on a Bicycle'!? Let me explain!

I have suffered for years with a bad stomach and have had various intolerances and allergies so I have often found myself in a desperate sweat, seeking out a toilet in a foreign place. From having to go in a field to using someone's house when I mistakenly thought it was the restaurant's facilities, I have had so many near misses and painful bad stomach experiences over the years. It's only in recent times that I have discovered this valuable piece of advice, quite by chance. I have also took the liberty of testing it out further to ensure that it is indeed true.

I had been on a bicycle ride in to the rural areas near where we were living in Phong Nha, Vietnam, and had cycled to a place that had barbecue chicken for our lunch. We had plenty of delicious food with a couple of beers and I completely forgot that beers do not sit well with my digestive system. I have a rule that if there is a chance to go to a toilet to always pay a visit before setting off, so I did and all was fine. After cycling for less than a couple of kilometres in the hot sun and being further away from any toilet, I got the signs all was not well. We have all had the feeling that we need to urgently go and that there was no time to waste. I expressed my discomfort to my partner who kindly pointed out that we were in the middle of a flat cycle ride with nowhere to go so I would just have to hold it. The pain came first, followed by the sweats, then the gurgles and the sheer fear that I was about to shit myself...on a bicycle. I called out to my fellow cyclist who was already ahead of me, possibly scouting out a tree or ditch! When I said that I was actually going to do it, he simply replied that I would be fine as long as I did not let my body leave the bike seat. He's a keen cyclist and a firm believer that you can't shit yourself on a bicycle and that the only course of action was to continue riding the bike. After what seemed like forever and me being barely able to see from the amount of sweat in my eyes, we arrived at a small roadside cafe. I was about to dismount, throw the bike down and run. I heard "No!!!! Don't get off the bike, yet!" And this was one of the best bits of advice as it was so true. I managed to cycle so close to the toilet door and as soon as the pressure of being sat on the bicycle seat had been removed, it felt like less than a second to get into position. I had come full circle and was back to that dreaded squat toilet, but now I was well versed in the use of such a WC.

Since then, if ever I am in a similar situation, I get on my bicycle, and ride as fast as I can to a place with a toilet that is easy to cycle extremely near to. I've even been known to borrow a bicycle if I haven't got mine, as this can also work in a desperate situation.

My life now has changed a little as I continue to help people who are travelling or are taking holidays, either abroad or in their own country. I've recently become a travel adviser for a company where holidays and trips are booked by a local resort expert (like me). Resort Experts prides itself on having people who live & work in the destinations you are travelling to so that we can offer insider tips and a personalised touch to make your holiday truly extraordinary.

I also continue to write a daily blog, the highs and lows of my everyday life and more handy travel tips are already on the way, but for now you have 12 eventualities to consider your solution should you get in to a predicament.

I'd love to hear of any predicaments that you find yourself in and any funny stories about them. Happy Travelling!

Useful Links:

My Blog can be found at https://joloyolo.com/

My Business Facebook page can be found here: https://www.facebook.com/profile.php?id=61567498001133

If you would like to discuss booking your next holiday with me, you will find me here: https://resort-experts.com/experts/jo-lomas/

Next Book Title:

You Can't Eat a whole Blancmange and Dance.....

..and other handy travel tips!

Printed in Great Britain
by Amazon